$2.00

Valentine's Day

Dennis Brindell Fradin

—Best Holiday Books—

ENSLOW PUBLISHERS, INC.

Bloy St. & Ramsey Ave.   P.O. Box 38

Box 777   Aldershot

Hillside, N.J. 07205   Hants GU12 6BP

U.S.A.   U.K.

> *For my wife, Judy, always my valentine*

Library of Congress Cataloging-in-Publication Data
Fradin, Dennis B.
   Valentine's Day / by Dennis Brindell Fradin.
      p. cm.—(Best holiday books)
   Includes index.
   Summary: Describes the history behind Valentine's Day and the various ways it is celebrated.

ISBN 0-89490-237-7

1. Valentine's Day—Juvenile literature. {1. Valentine's Day.} I. Title. II. Series: Fradin, Dennis B. Best holiday books.

GT4925.F73 1990
394.2'683—dc20   89-7682
                                                        CIP
                                                        AC

Printed in the United States of America

10 9 8 7 6 5 4 3 2 1

Illustration Credits:
Courtesy, American Antiquarian Society: p. 28; American Greetings Corporation: p. 37; Cameramann International, Ltd.: pp. 4, 8, 33, 37, 40; Tom Dunnington: pp. 11, 21; Historical Pictures Service, Chicago: pp. 14, 18, 31; Hallmark Cards, Inc.: pp. 17, 36, 41, 44; Library of Congress: pp. 22, 27; Norma Morrison: p. 12; Evalene Pulati, president, National Valentine Collectors Association: pp. 24, 29.

Cover Illustration by Charlott Nathan.

Contents

Children enjoy making valentines at school.

A Day for Hearts and Flowers

It happens every year in early February. Children make cards at school. They draw hearts and flowers on the cards. They write "Be My Valentine" on them. On February 14— Valentine's Day—they give the cards to friends and relatives.

Valentine's Day is not a legal holiday. Schools and offices are open. There is mail. But it is a special day when people of all ages show their love for others.

The cards given on Valentine's Day are called valentines. Many people, especially children, make their valentines. Other people buy valentines and write messages on them.

The Roots of Valentine's Day

The roots of Valentine's Day go back many hundreds of years. Exactly how it began is not known. But there are four main ideas.

First Idea: The Roman Lupercalia. Over 2,000 years ago, people in ancient Rome held a religious rite called the Lupercalia. It took place on February 15. As part of the Lupercalia, young women let themselves be whipped with goatskins. They thought this would please the gods. In return, the gods would help the women have children.

The Lupercalia may have had a gentler side that wasn't part of the religious ceremonies. Some think that on February 14, Roman women wrote their names on paper. The names went into a bowl. On the night of February 14, young men drew the names. The woman whose name a man pulled would be his partner at dances for the year.

These rites may have started Valentine's Day. The name drawings (if they occurred) may have begun the custom of drawing valentines from a box. The idea that the rites helped women have children fits in with Valentine's Day too. Many people get married on Valentine's Day. And marriage often leads to having children!

Second Idea: Two Saint Valentines. A second idea says that a priest (or priests) named Valentine began the holiday. The time was about 270 A.D., meaning about 270 years after Christ's birth. The Romans were jailing and killing Christians. The Romans were angry that people were giving up the Roman gods to become Christians.

Claudius II, the Roman king, needed soldiers. Married men wanted to stay with their

The custom of taking valentines from a container may have begun with the Romans.

families instead of becoming soldiers. So Claudius made a law that young men could not marry. A priest who married a couple would be killed.

A priest named Valentine was said to have ignored this law and secretly married young men and women. Claudius II found out and arrested him. On February 14 of about the year 270 A.D., Valentine was put to death in Rome.

Valentine was later named a Christian saint. And since he had helped lovers, he was remembered in a loving way. February 14—the day he died—became a day for people to express love for each other.

There was also a story about a second Valentine, who was known for his love of children. Claudius II jailed him for helping Christians who were oppressed by the Romans. The king told Valentine he could live if he gave up Christianity. Valentine refused and was sentenced to die.

The children missed Valentine. They threw him notes through his jail window. During his last days, Valentine befriended a blind girl who brought him food. By a miracle, Valentine made her see again. This Valentine was also reportedly put to death on February 14 of about the year 270 A.D. Just before he died, Valentine sent a note to the girl who had brought him food. He signed it "From your Valentine."

Like the other Valentine, this man was also made a saint. And the day he sent his last loving note—February 14—became a day for people to send loving messages.

There could have been two Saint Valentines. And both could have died in Rome on February 14 of the same year. But some think there was just one Valentine. He married people, loved children, helped Christians, and sent the girl the note. People may have become confused over the years and thought there were two.

Third Idea: The Day the Birds Mate. Hundreds of years ago, Europeans noticed something about birds. Some birds pick their mates about February 14. This inspired a wrong

Children throwing notes through the bars of Valentine's window

It was once widely thought that all birds chose their mates on February 14.

idea. People decided that *all* birds mate *on* February 14.

Since birds supposedly paired up on February 14, the idea developed that people should, too. It became a day for young men and women to show interest in each other.

Fourth Idea: All of the Above. All of the above ideas could be true. The Roman Lupercalia may have been the beginning of Valentine's Day. The death of one or two Saint Valentines may have inspired the sending of love tokens on February 14. The idea that birds mate on that day may have helped the custom take root.

Saint Valentine

Early Valentine's Day Customs

The giving of valentines is the main Valentine's Day custom today. There is no proof that people did this until the 1400s. Before then, people may not have done anything special on Valentine's Day.

In late 1415, England defeated France in the Battle of Agincourt. The Frenchman Charles, Duke of Orleans, was captured. He was locked in the Tower of London. Charles missed his wife. Around Valentine's Day of 1416 he wrote her some love poems. They are the first known Valentine's Day messages. Other Valentine's Day poems and letters from the 1400s, 1500s, and 1600s have also been found.

Other European nations besides England and France also honored Valentine's Day. The day was observed in various ways in Italy, Scotland, Wales, Denmark, Germany, and the Netherlands. In Italy, for example, young people met in gardens on February 14. They listened to poems and music. But England was where Valentine's Day grew into the holiday we know.

By the 1600s, England had some interesting Valentine's Day customs. Many English girls believed they would marry the first boy they saw on February 14. They kept their eyes closed until a boy they liked came by. Then they went to the window to see him.

Name drawing was another English Valentine's Day custom. Slips of paper with names on them went into a box. Males drew names of girls and women. Females drew names of boys and men. This became a way to bring shy people together. It was often arranged for people to draw the names of those they secretly liked. The two people were "valentines" for the next year. This

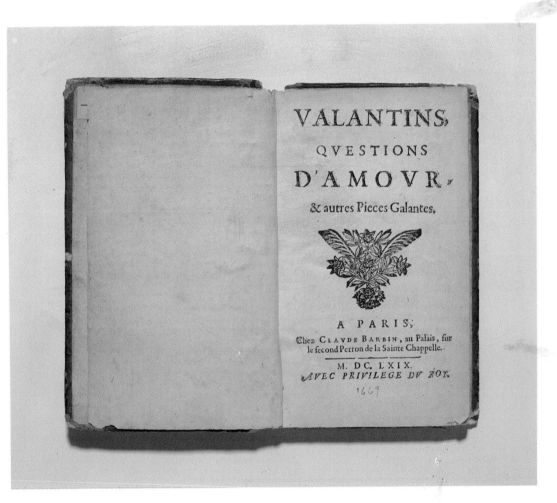

A book on valentines and love published in Paris in 1669

Young Englishwoman accepting a gift from the first person she has seen on Valentine's Day. Since her eyes were closed, perhaps he called out that he was there.

meant that they spent time together and in many cases exchanged fancy gifts.

The name drawing did not always lead to romance. Sometimes a young boy would be paired with a woman, or a young girl with an older man. They would simply be friends for the year.

The first known decorated valentine was made by a boy for a woman. The year was 1667, and the place was London, England. Young Will Mercer drew Mrs. Elizabeth Pepys as his valentine. Will made a gold and blue valentine. He gave it to Mrs. Pepys on Valentine's Day morning.

This was unusual for those years. Until about 1750 most Valentine's Day gifts were costly. People who could not afford fancy gifts were left out of the holiday.

Valentine's Day Becomes More Popular

Valentine's Day slowly changed in the early 1700s. Fewer people gave costly gifts. But more people sent messages of love. Handmade valentine cards like Will Mercer's became more popular. Since the valentines cost little to make, more people took part in Valentine's Day.

By the mid-1700s, Americans were also making and giving valentines. People from England and Germany brought the custom to America.

A big change in Valentine's Day took place in about 1800. Before then, valentines were made by hand. Starting around 1800, machine-printed valentines became popular. People

Women making valentines in a factory during the 1800s

bought these valentines from printers. There was room on them for a personal message.

"Valentine Writers" also became popular around 1800. These booklets contained poems by authors. A Valentine Writer cost a penny. People who were not good writers copied the poems onto their valentines.

Magazine illustration from 1859 showing ladies and a girl greeting the mailman on Valentine's Day

By 1830 a new type of valentine was becoming popular. This was the "comic valentine." Many of today's valentines are funny. But many comic valentines of the 1800s were cruel. They made fun of the way people looked or acted. Sending them was a way to hurt someone the sender did not like.

Before the mid-1800s, few people sent valentines long distances. Mail services were expensive. Mail often took weeks to go from one city to another.

During the 1840s, Great Britain and the United States created better, cheaper mail services. People began sending valentines to loved ones in far-off cities. Valentine's Day is still one of the year's busiest days for mail in some countries.

A valentine dating from about 1880, during the "Golden Age"

The "Golden Age" of Valentines

The years from the 1840s to the late 1890s were the "Golden Age" of valentines. Many valentines made during those years were works of art.

In England the husband and wife Jonathan and Clarissa King made lovely valentines. Around 1850, Clarissa King became the first person to put feathers and glitter on valentines. She ground up colored glass to make glitter. The King family built a factory. Several dozen people worked there making valentines.

Esther Howland (1828–1904) was the most famous valentine maker of the Golden Age. Esther Howland lived in Worcester, Massachusetts. Her father ran a store where he sold books and paper goods. Each February he sold fancy valentines from Europe. In about 1848, Esther decided that she could make prettier valentines than the European ones.

Esther made a few valentines. They soon sold out in the shop. Esther then made more valentines and sold them to stores in Boston and New York. The store owners loved them! They asked her for a large supply of valentines for the next year.

Esther Howland set up a business in her home. She designed the valentines. She hired young women to put them together. One woman cut out the pictures for the valentines. Another pasted on the pictures and paper flowers. Yet another attached the lace.

Most Howland Company valentines cost from $5 to $10. Some were over $30—a fortune back then. Yet each year she sold thousands of valentines. Some years she sold $100,000 worth. By the 1870s, she also made Christmas and other kinds of cards.

Esther Howland was the valentine queen. But other artistic people also made names for themselves during this period. Among them was the Englishwoman Kate Greenaway (1846–1901). Early in her career, Kate Greenaway earned

Kate Greenaway

money by designing valentines and Christmas cards. Later she became a famous children's book illustrator.

An Esther Howland valentine

This beautiful valentine dates from about 1920.

The 1900s

By the early 1900s, people in England and the United States were losing interest in valentines. They had become too expensive for most people. For a while, it looked as though the sending of valentines would die out.

Then, between 1906 and 1919, several big greeting card companies were started. Among them were American Greetings, Hallmark, and Norcross. These companies sold pretty cards at a low cost. For the price of one Esther Howland card, a person could buy dozens of cards.

People became interested in Valentine's Day again. Children began buying enough cards for all their friends. Today children are the main givers of valentines. And although Germany,

France, Spain, Denmark, and Italy also observe Valentine's Day, the United States and Great Britain are still the main nations that honor the holiday.

Children looking at valentines on a bulletin board in the early 1900s

Schoolchildren and Valentine's Day

Each year, millions of children do Valentine's Day projects at school. Their teachers pass out paper, crayons, scissors, lace, and paste. The children use these to make their valentines.

Many children decorate their valentines with hearts, flowers, birds, and arrows. These are symbols of the holiday. In other words, they make people think of Valentine's Day.

Do you know why children often decorate their valentines with heart-shaped designs? People once thought that the heart produced feelings of love. The fact is that our brains create our feelings. But the heart is still a symbol of love.

Children still make valentines more than 300 years after a child made the first known decorated valentine.

And the heart's color—red—is a special Valentine's Day color.

Do you know why many children decorate their valentines with flowers and birds? Valentine's Day comes just before spring begins, so people are thinking about flowers and birds. The bird decorations are also a holdover from the idea that birds mate on February 14.

Some children draw arrows through hearts on their valentines. A heart with arrows has been a symbol of love for centuries. Few people know the reason.

The Romans had a god of love named Cupid. He had a magic bow and arrows. Anyone the little god shot with an arrow fell in love. This old myth about Cupid inspired the use of arrows on valentines.

On Valentine's Day itself, many teachers hold class parties. Valentines are usually exchanged at these parties. Most teachers say that, if you give valentines in class, you must give them to everyone. That way no one feels left out.

Sometimes the valentines are placed in a big box and then passed out by several students. The valentine box is like the name drawing that English and perhaps Roman people did long ago.

Food is served at many school Valentine's Day parties. The teachers and children may bring heart-shaped candy or cookies to the parties. Some children dress in special ways for their school Valentine's Day parties. Girls may wear heart-shaped earrings and red dresses. Boys may wear red shirts and socks.

Flowers have long been important Valentine's Day symbols. This valentine dates from about the year 1900.

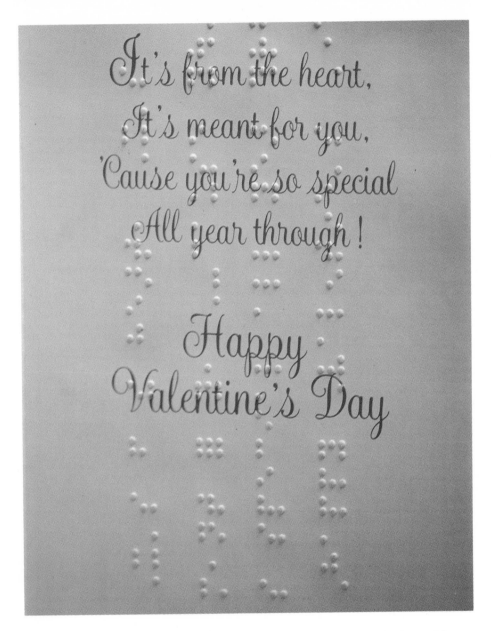

It's from the heart,
It's meant for you,
'Cause you're so special
All year through !

Happy
Valentine's Day

This valentine is in Braille, a special code for the blind. Braille is read by feeling the raised dots.

Teens and Adults Like Valentine's Day, Too!

Children aren't the only ones who like Valentine's Day. Older people from teens to senior citizens also enjoy it. Many of these people like to send valentines as much as children do. Some husbands and wives borrow their children's crayons and make each other valentines. A teenage boy who is too shy to speak to a girl may send her a valentine. That way the letter carrier does the work, and the girl gets the message.

Teens and adults like Valentine's Day parties, too. Many schools and community centers hold Valentine's Day dances. Some adults hold

Valentine's Day parties in their homes. And some businesses offer Valentine's Day treats to their workers on February 14.

Many sweethearts and married people exchange Valentine's Day gifts. Candy in heart-shaped boxes is a popular Valentine's Day gift. A woman might give a man a book or even socks with little hearts on them. A man might give a woman flowers. Red roses are popular Valentine's Day gifts in the United States. In Denmark white flowers called snowdrops are popular. Danish people place snowdrops on poems they send friends around Valentine's Day.

Some adults place special Valentine's Day messages to their loved ones in newspapers. They must pay for these ads. The ads are often short rhymes that start with such lines as "Roses are red, and violets are blue . . ." and end with the words, "I love you." Others are simple messages like "Sue—I love you with all my ♥ ."

Det er ikke an leg
Naar jeg siger
"Jeg elsker dig"

Kan du gætte hvem?

In Denmark, people send a valentine with a joke and flowers called snowdrops on it.

This 1944 valentine was made during World War II.

People who place these ads often use nicknames like "From Poopsie to Honey Bunch." Reading the Valentine's Day ads on February 14 is a lot of fun. It reminds us that millions of people love each other, which is what Valentine's Day is all about!

One Problem With Valentine's Day

People get a lot of pleasure from Valentine's Day. Parents are reminded of their children's love on this day. Husbands and wives exchange tokens of love. And children are thrilled when friends give them valentines.

There is just one problem with this day of hearts, flowers, and love. It comes only once a year! On other days, many of us do not show people that we love or like them. By letting people know that we care for them, we can put a bit of Valentine's Day into every day of the year.

An Esther Howland valentine

Glossary

Cupid—the Romans' god of love

custom—a way of doing things that people teach their children

dozen—twelve

expensive—costly

illustrator—someone who does artwork that goes along with a printed work

Lupercalia—a Roman religious rite that may have started Valentine's Day

million—a thousand thousand (1,000,000)

miracle—an amazing event that is thought to show God's will

oppressed—mistreated

rites—religious ceremonies

saint—a very holy person

snowdrops—a kind of white flower

sweethearts—people who are in love

symbols—things that make us think of other things; a red heart is a symbol of Valentine's Day

B Battle of Agincourt, 15
birds and Valentine's Day, 10, 13, 34

C Charles, Duke of Orleans, 15
Claudius II, 7, 9
Cupid, 34
customs, 5, 15-19, 38-42

D Denmark, 16, 31, 39

E England, 15, 16, 19, 20, 23, 25, 30, 31

F flowers, 5, 32, 34, 39, 43
France, 15, 16, 31

G Germany, 16, 30
Great Britain. *See* England.
Greenaway, Kate, 27-28

H Howland, Esther, 25-27, 30

I Italy, 16, 31

K King, Jonathan and Clarissa, 25